READY TO LEARN

First Grade

1²3 Math
Workbook

Table of Contents

First Grade Math Readiness

Parents and caregivers are a child's first and most important teachers. Help your child be successful by talking about math in his or her daily life. Choose games and activities that incorporate adding and subtracting. Talk about things like how long until dinnertime or soccer practice. Teach them that math is important and fun!

Vocabulary Builder

Plus	+	the word and symbol for adding
Minus	–	the word and symbol for subtracting
Greater than	>	
Less than	<	
Equals	=	

Number Sense

Writing Numbers 1-10

Trace and then practice writing the numbers on the lines below.

1   1

2   2

3   3

4   4

5   5

6   6

7   7

8   8

9   9

10   10

Number Sense

Counting 1-10

Count the pictures in each box and write the total number on the lines below.

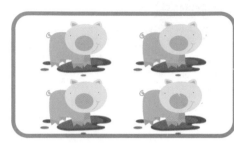 _4_

 _____

 _2_

 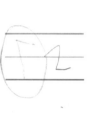

 _____

 _9_

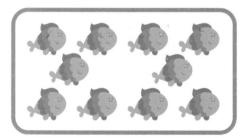  _3_

 _5_

 _____

Number Sense

Writing Numbers 11-20

Trace and then practice writing the numbers on the lines below.

11 11

12 12

13 13

14 14

15 15

16 16

17 17

18 18

19 19

20 20

Counting 11-20

Count the pictures in each box and write the total number on the lines below.

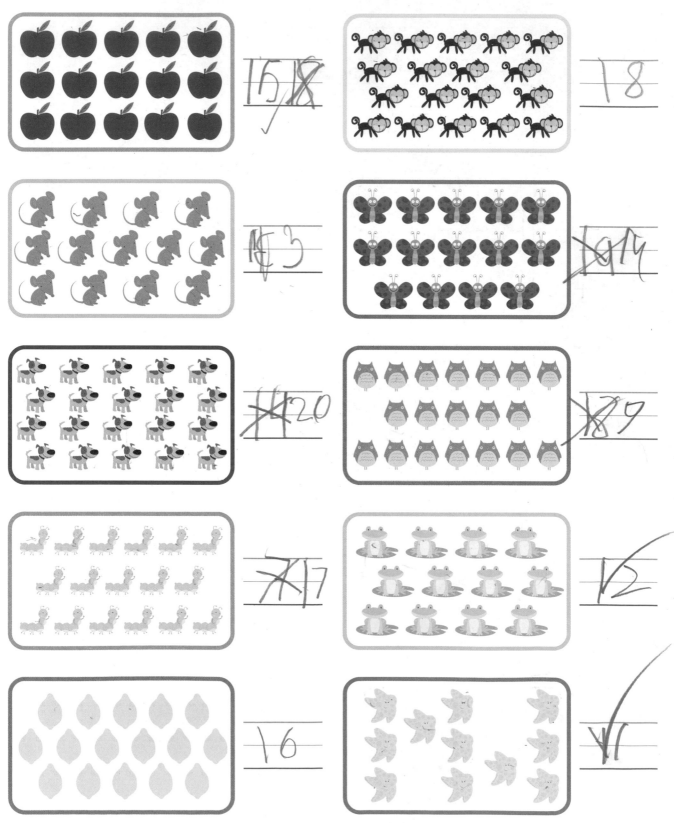

Number Words

Draw a line from the number word to the matching number.

one	3
two	4
three	1
four	2
five	7
six	5
seven	8
eight	6
nine	10
ten	9

Number Sense

Count to 50

Write the missing numbers on the snake.

Color it in when you're finished.

Number Sense

Counting 51-100

Connect the dots from 51 to 100.

Color your new friend when you're finished.

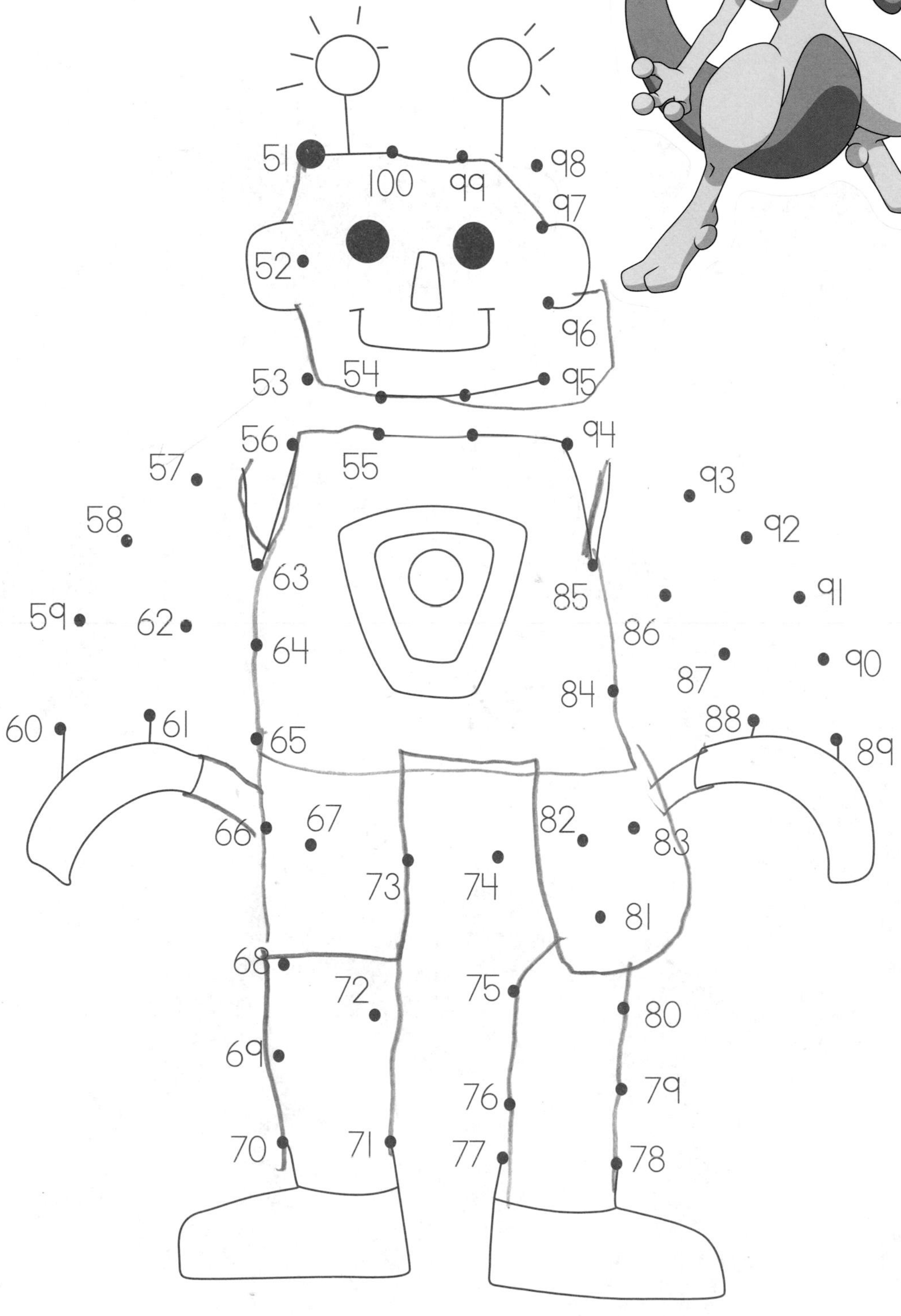

51 98
100 99 97
52
53 54 95
96
56 94
55
57 93
58 92
85 91
63 86
64 84 87 90
59 62 88 89
60 61 65
82 83
66 67 81
73 74
68 80
72 75
69 79
76
70 71 77 78

Race to 100

Write the missing numbers in each square to reach 100.

Race 1 to 100

1	2	3	4	5	6	7	8	9	10
11	12	13	14	15	16	17	18	19	20
21	22	23	24	25	26	27	28		30
31	32	33	34	35	36	38	39		
40	41	42	46	47	48		49		50
51	52	53	54	55	56	57		59	
61									
									100

Count by Twos

Skip counting can make counting faster! Skip counting **means** skipping numbers as you count.

Circle groups of 2 objects while you skip count the pictures in each row. Write the number on the lines for how many you counted in each row.

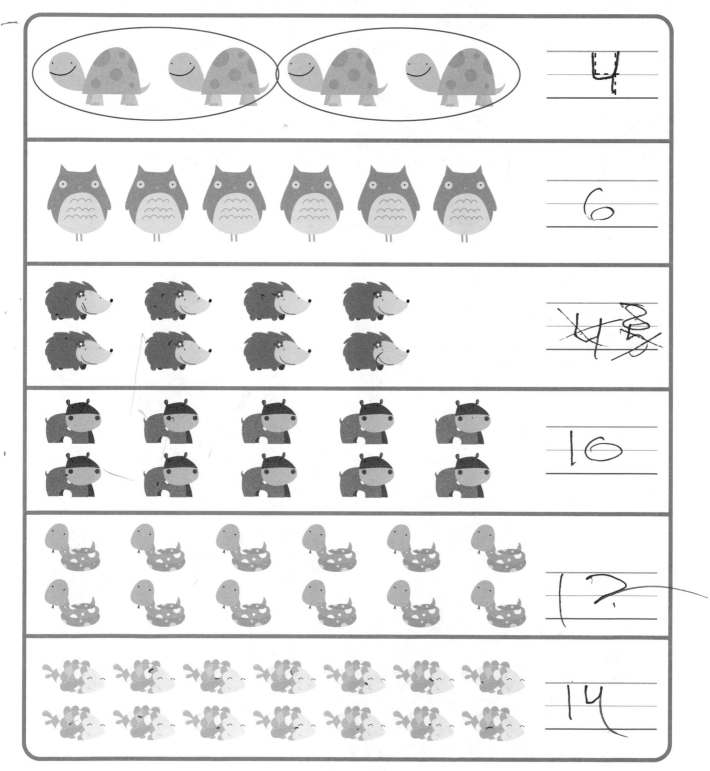

Count by Fives

Skip count by 5 up to 100 and write the missing numbers on the hands below.

Number Sense

Count by Tens

Count 10 objects at a time. Circle sets of 10 objects while you skip count the objects in each row. Write the number on the lines for how many you counted in each row.

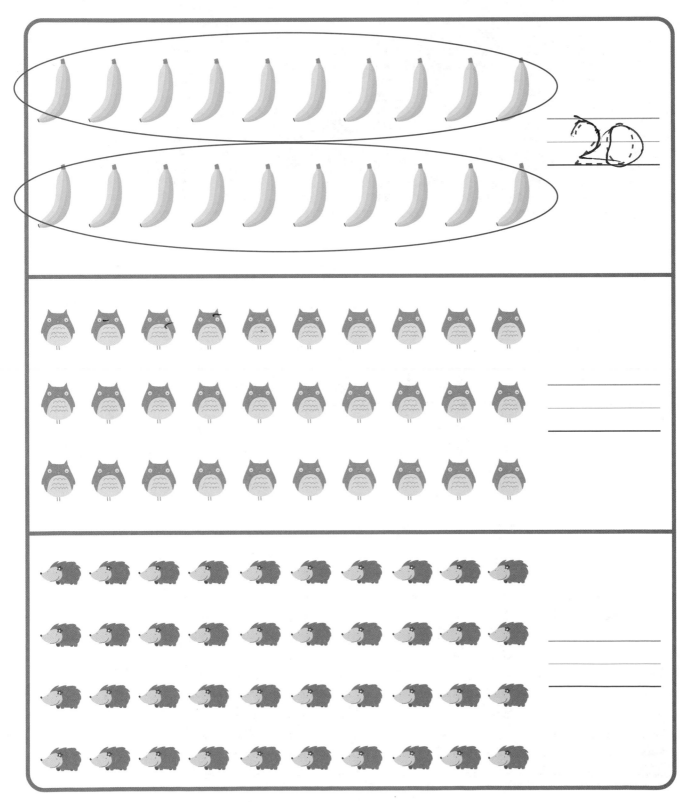

Number Sense

Count by Tens

Count 10 objects at a time. Circle sets of 10 objects while you skip count the pictures in each row. Write the number on the lines for how many you counted in each row.

Addition

Practice Addition

Count the objects in each box and write the numbers in the equations. Write the sum after the equals sign.

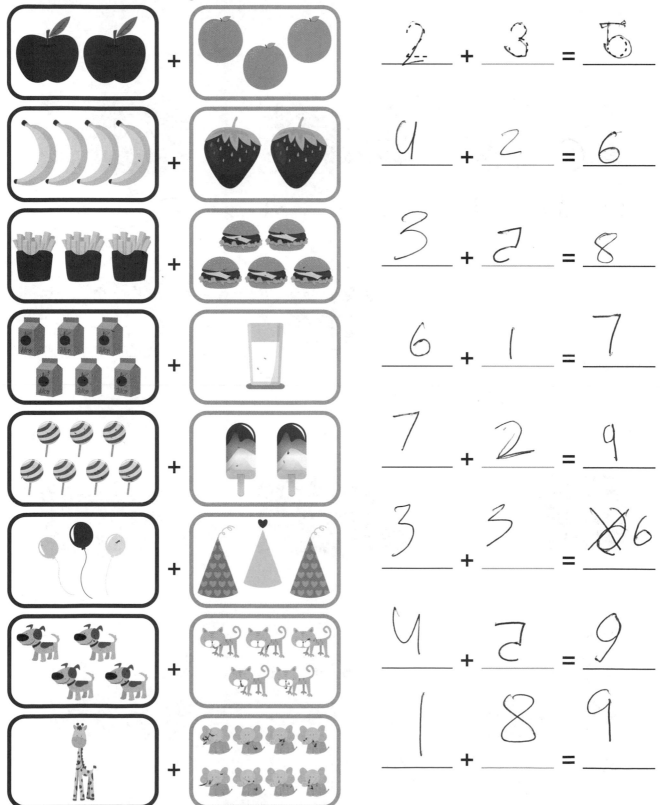

$2 + 3 = 5$

$4 + 2 = 6$

$3 + 2 = 8$

$6 + 1 = 7$

$7 + 2 = 9$

$3 + 3 = 6$

$4 + 2 = 9$

$1 + 8 = 9$

15

Addition

Let's Play Dominoes!

Count the dots in each side of the domino and write the numbers in the equations. Write the sum after the equals sign.

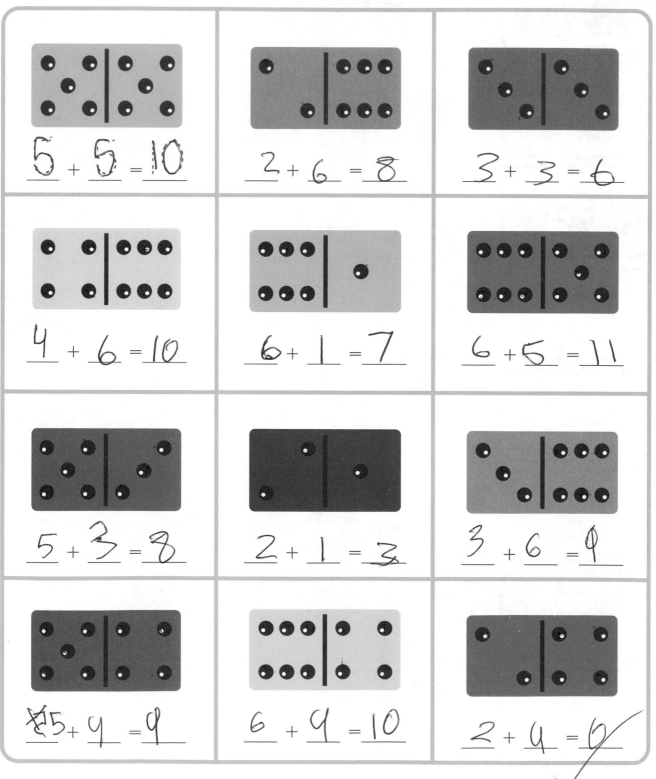

5 + 5 = 10

2 + 6 = 8

3 + 3 = 6

4 + 6 = 10

6 + 1 = 7

6 + 5 = 11

5 + 3 = 8

2 + 1 = 3

3 + 6 = 9

5 + 4 = 9

6 + 4 = 10

2 + 4 = 6

16

Addition

Vertical Equations

Count the red and green apples for each addition equation. Write the sum below each equals line.

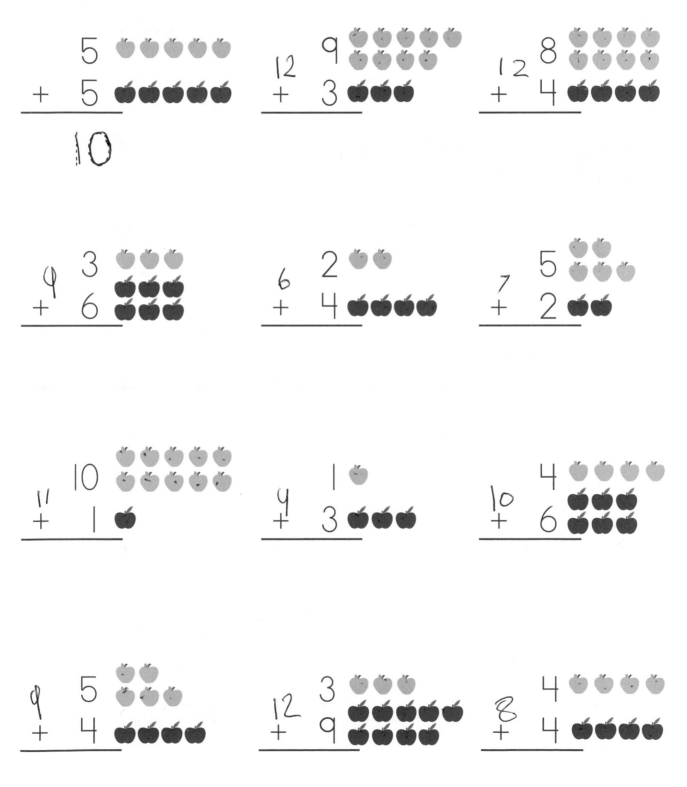

$\begin{array}{r} 5 \\ + 5 \\ \hline 10 \end{array}$

$\begin{array}{r} 12 \quad 9 \\ + 3 \\ \hline \end{array}$

$\begin{array}{r} 12 \quad 8 \\ + 4 \\ \hline \end{array}$

$\begin{array}{r} 9 \quad 3 \\ + 6 \\ \hline \end{array}$

$\begin{array}{r} 6 \quad 2 \\ + 4 \\ \hline \end{array}$

$\begin{array}{r} 7 \quad 5 \\ + 2 \\ \hline \end{array}$

$\begin{array}{r} 11 \quad 10 \\ + 1 \\ \hline \end{array}$

$\begin{array}{r} 4 \quad 1 \\ + 3 \\ \hline \end{array}$

$\begin{array}{r} 10 \quad 4 \\ + 6 \\ \hline \end{array}$

$\begin{array}{r} 9 \quad 5 \\ + 4 \\ \hline \end{array}$

$\begin{array}{r} 12 \quad 3 \\ + 9 \\ \hline \end{array}$

$\begin{array}{r} 8 \quad 4 \\ + 4 \\ \hline \end{array}$

Using a Number Line

You can use a number line to help you count when adding.

Start on the number line at the first number in the equation. Then jump forward the number of spaces for the amount being added to the first number. Circle the number on the number line where the jump line ends. This is the sum. Write the sum after the equals sign.

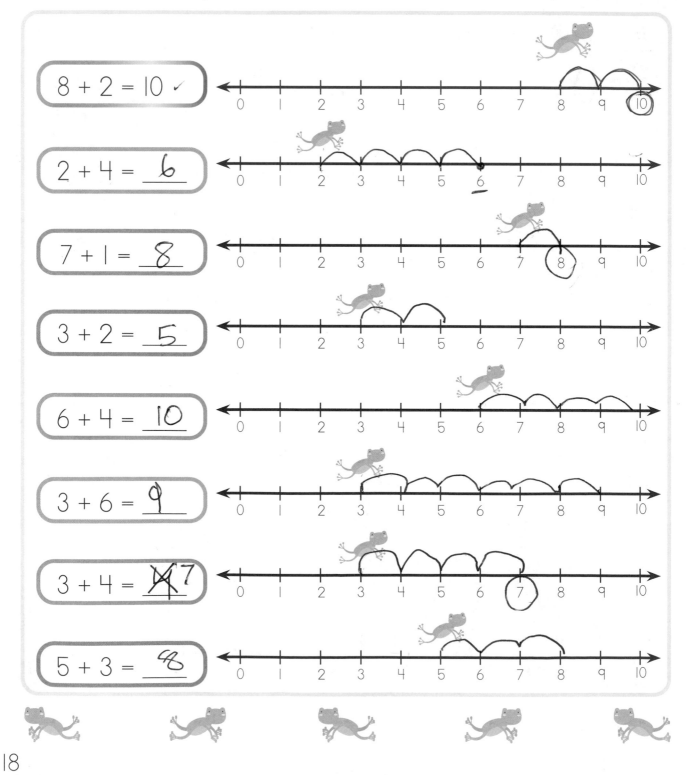

$8 + 2 = 10$ ✓

$2 + 4 = \underline{6}$

$7 + 1 = \underline{8}$

$3 + 2 = \underline{5}$

$6 + 4 = \underline{10}$

$3 + 6 = \underline{9}$

$3 + 4 = \underline{7}$

$5 + 3 = \underline{8}$

Addition

Using a Number Line

Start on the first number in the equation. Then jump forward on the line the same number of spaces as the second number. Draw a line from the first number to the second number and circle the correct answer. Then write the answers to the equations on the lines below.

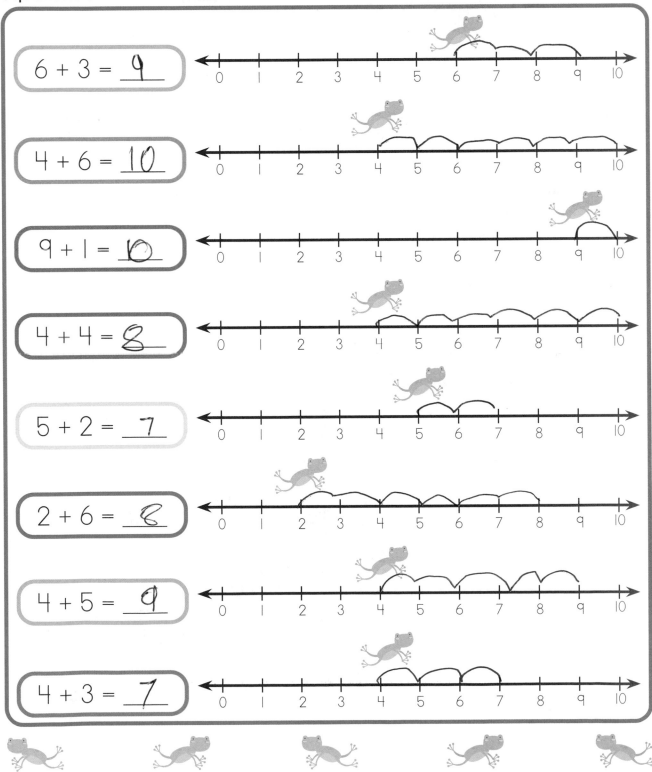

$6 + 3 =$ ___9___

$4 + 6 =$ ___10___

$9 + 1 =$ ___10___

$4 + 4 =$ ___8___

$5 + 2 =$ ___7___

$2 + 6 =$ ___8___

$4 + 5 =$ ___9___

$4 + 3 =$ ___7___

Sunny Summer Math

Solve the addition equations and write the sums on the lines below. Then color the pictures.

4 + 8 = ___   4 + 6 = ___   5 + 6 = ___

9 + 3 = ___   6 + 6 = ___   5 + 7 = ___

9 + 1 = ___   5 + 1 = ___   8 + 3 = ___

7 + 5 = ___   9 + 2 = ___   7 + 4 = ___

6 + 2 = ___   1 + 6 = ___   6 + 3 = ___   10 + 2 = ___

11 + 1 = ___   4 + 4 = ___   8 + 5 = ___   3 + 8 = ___

20

Addition

Word Problems

Sometimes math equations are hidden in word problems. Read each addition word problem carefully and figure out the unknown number to solve the equation. Write that number on the line in each equation.

Example: Maddy has ②red beads. She got ③more beads from a friend. How many beads does Maddy have now?

$$2 + 3 = \underline{5}$$

Circle the clues and solve the word problems. Write your answers on the lines below.

1. Lucy has a seashell collection. She was given 3 more seashells. Now she has 10 seashells. How many seashells did she have before she got some more?

$$\underline{\quad} + 3 = 10$$

2. Emma invites 10 children to her party. Some girls and 5 boys came. How many girls were invited?

$$5 + \underline{\quad} = 10$$

3. Sophia likes to run. She runs 4 miles on Monday and 6 miles on Tuesday. How far did she run in two days?

$$4 + 6 = \underline{\quad}$$

4. Noah has 2 toy trucks. Luke has 7 toy trucks. How many more toy trucks does Luke have than Noah?

$$2 + \underline{\quad} = 7$$

Addition

Add to the Fun

Solve the addition problems. Write the answers below.

```
2   2        4   3        8   2        6   3        7   2
  + 0          + 1          + 6          + 3          + 5
```

```
8   7        9   6        10  1        11  5        10 10
  + 1          + 3          + 9          + 6          + 2
                                         11
```

```
7   5        8   3        9   4        7   0        9   5
  + 7          + 8          + 5          + 7          + 4
```

```
12  8        7   3
  + 4          + 7
```

```
12  7        10  5
  + 5          + 5
```

```
9   0        8   4
  + 9          + 1
```

22

Word Problems

Read each addition word problem carefully and figure out the unknown number to solve the equation. Write that number on the line in each equation.

1. Sarah has 5 test tubes. She has 3 yellow and the rest are red. How many test tubes are red?

$$3 + \underline{\quad} = 5$$

2. Lauren has 4 T-shirts with a red heart on them. She has 5 T-shirts with a dog on them. How many T-shirts does she own?

$$4 + 5 = \underline{\quad}$$

3. Ashley has 8 shoes. She has 6 shoes with laces and the rest have buttons. How many shoes have buttons?

$$6 + \underline{\quad} = 8$$

4. Kim painted all 10 of her nails. She painted 3 pink and the rest she painted blue. How many nails did she paint blue?

$$\underline{\quad} + 3 = 10$$

Counting Backward

Counting backward helps you learn how to subtract numbers. Count backward by 1s and write the missing numbers in each caterpillar sequence as you count. Then color the caterpillars.

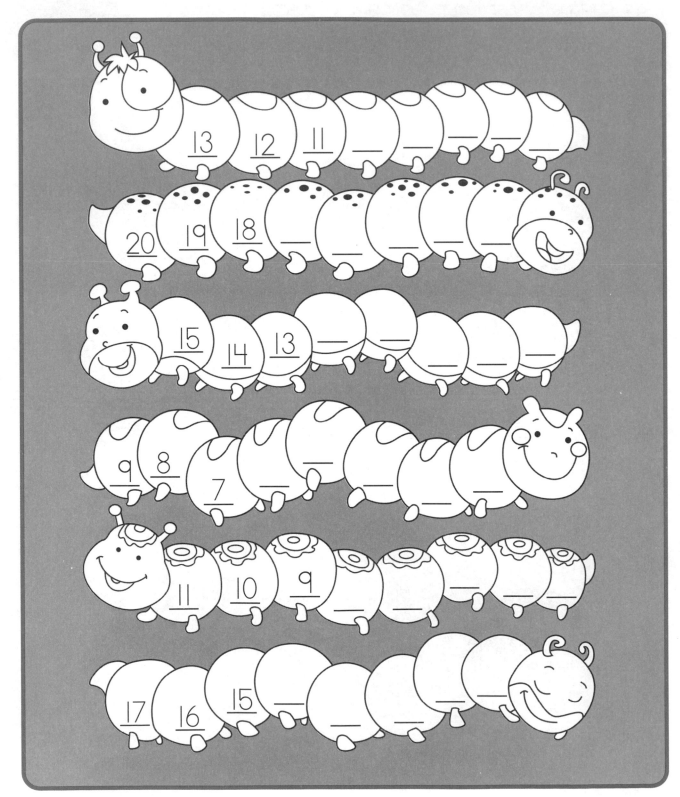

Subtraction

Practice Subtraction

Subtracting is taking away part of a whole number.

When we use pictures to subtract, we start with the whole number and then cross out the number of objects we are subtracting.

Example: $6 - 2 = 4$

Count the total number of objects in each row. Count backward for the amount of the second number in the equation which will be the x objects. The number of objects left is the difference. Write the difference under the equals line.

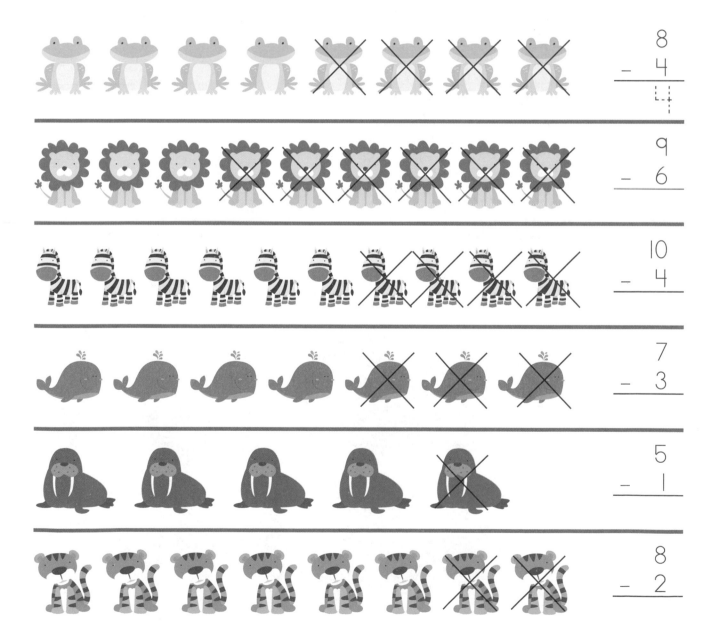

$$\begin{array}{r} 8 \\ -\ 4 \\ \hline 4 \end{array}$$

$$\begin{array}{r} 9 \\ -\ 6 \\ \hline \end{array}$$

$$\begin{array}{r} 10 \\ -\ 4 \\ \hline \end{array}$$

$$\begin{array}{r} 7 \\ -\ 3 \\ \hline \end{array}$$

$$\begin{array}{r} 5 \\ -\ 1 \\ \hline \end{array}$$

$$\begin{array}{r} 8 \\ -\ 2 \\ \hline \end{array}$$

Practice Subtraction

Cross out the number of objects you are subtracting from the total. Count the objects left and write the difference after the equals sign.

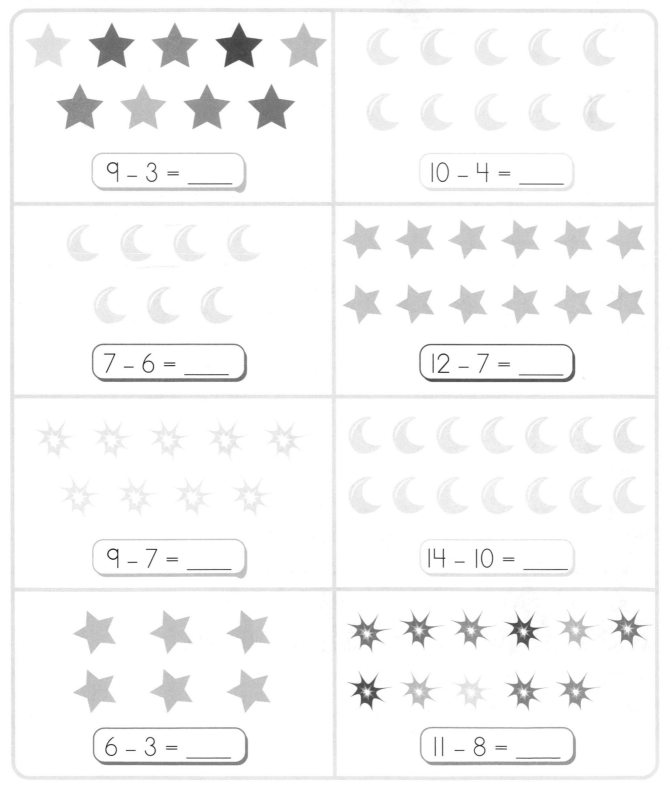

9 – 3 = _____

10 – 4 = _____

7 – 6 = _____

12 – 7 = _____

9 – 7 = _____

14 – 10 = _____

6 – 3 = _____

11 – 8 = _____

Subtraction

Practice Subtraction

Cross out the number of objects you are subtracting from the total. Count the objects left and write the difference after the equals sign.

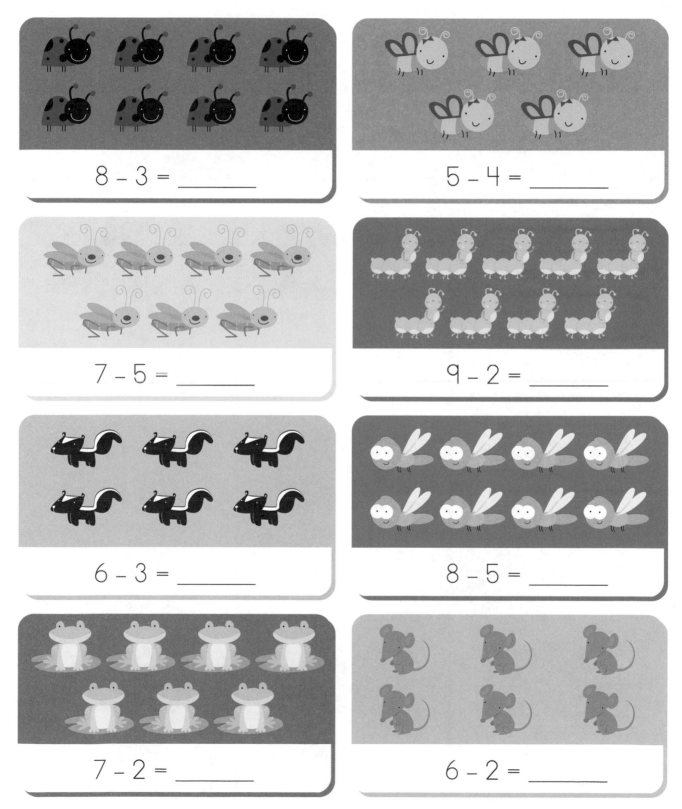

8 – 3 = _____

5 – 4 = _____

7 – 5 = _____

9 – 2 = _____

6 – 3 = _____

8 – 5 = _____

7 – 2 = _____

6 – 2 = _____

Subtraction

Let's Play Dominoes!

Use the dots on the dominoes to help you subtract. Write the difference for each equation after the equals sign.

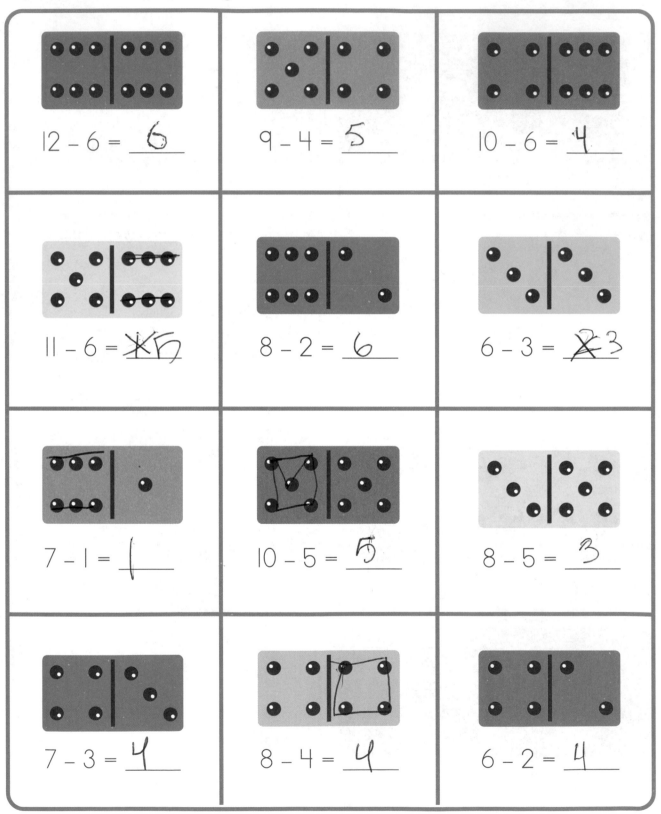

12 – 6 = 6

9 – 4 = 5

10 – 6 = 4

11 – 6 = 5

8 – 2 = 6

6 – 3 = 3

7 – 1 = 1

10 – 5 = 5

8 – 5 = 3

7 – 3 = 4

8 – 4 = 4

6 – 2 = 4

Subtraction

Word Problems

Sometimes math equations are hidden in word problems. Read each subtraction word problem carefully and figure out the unknown number to solve the equation. Write that number on the line in each equation.

Example: Maddy said there were (5) apples on the table. She ate some. Now there are (2) apples. How many did Maddy eat?

5 - _3_ = 2

Circle the clues and solve the word problems. Write your answers on the lines below.

1. Juan has 5 trading cards. He gave 2 away as gifts. How many does he still have?

$$5 - 2 = \underline{3}$$

2. Oliver popped 4 balloons at the party. Mason popped 8 balloons. How many fewer balloons did Oliver pop than Mason?

$$8 - 4 = \underline{4}$$

3. Logan has some drums on Monday. He gave 5 drums away on Tuesday. Now he has 4 drums. How many drums did he have on Monday?

$$\underline{9} - 5 = 4$$

4. Hannah has 4 fewer sheep than Riley. Riley has 7 sheep. How many sheep does Hannah have?

$$7 - 4 = \underline{3}$$

Using a Number Line

You can use a number line to help you count when subtracting.

Start on the number line at the first number in the equation. Then, jump backward the number of spaces for the amount being taken away from the first number. Circle the number on the number line where the jump line ends. This is the difference. Write the difference after the equals sign.

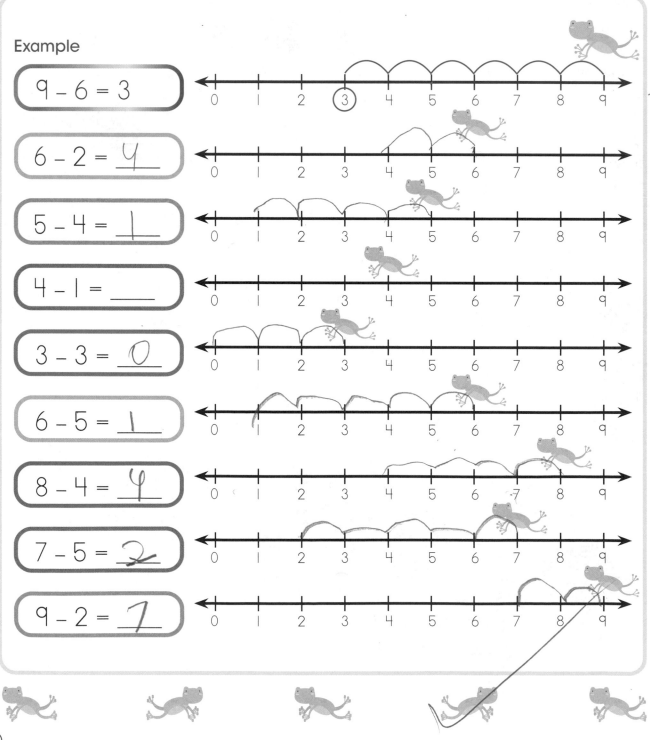

Example

9 – 6 = 3

6 – 2 = 4

5 – 4 = 1

4 – 1 = ___

3 – 3 = 0

6 – 5 = 1

8 – 4 = 4

7 – 5 = 2

9 – 2 = 7

Subtraction

Using a Number Line

Start on the number line at the first number in the equation. Then, jump backward the number of spaces for the amount being taken away from the first number. Circle the number on the number line where the jump line ends. This is the difference. Write the difference after the equals sign.

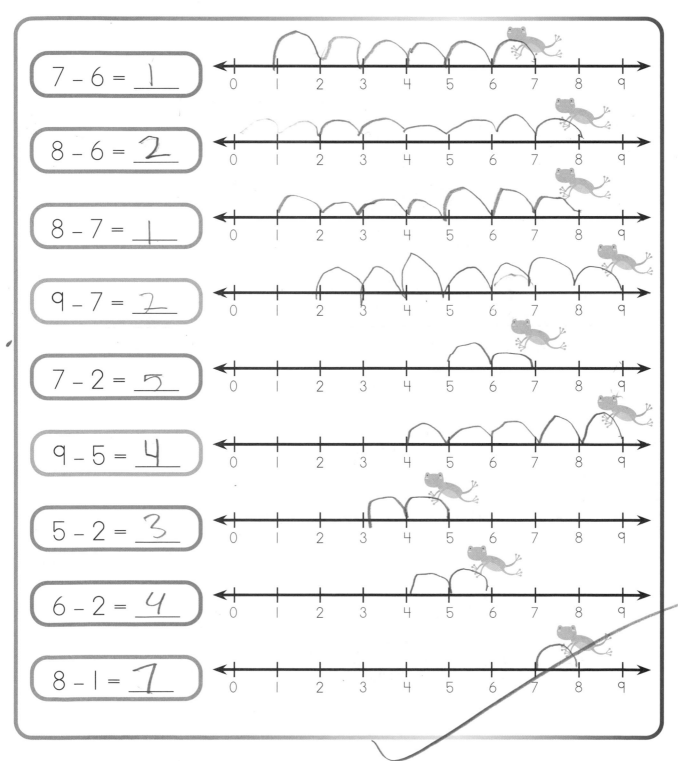

7 – 6 = 1

8 – 6 = 2

8 – 7 = 1

9 – 7 = 2

7 – 2 = 5

9 – 5 = 4

5 – 2 = 3

6 – 2 = 4

8 – 1 = 7

Subtraction

Math Can Be a Picnic!

Solve the subtraction equations and write the differences after the equals signs.

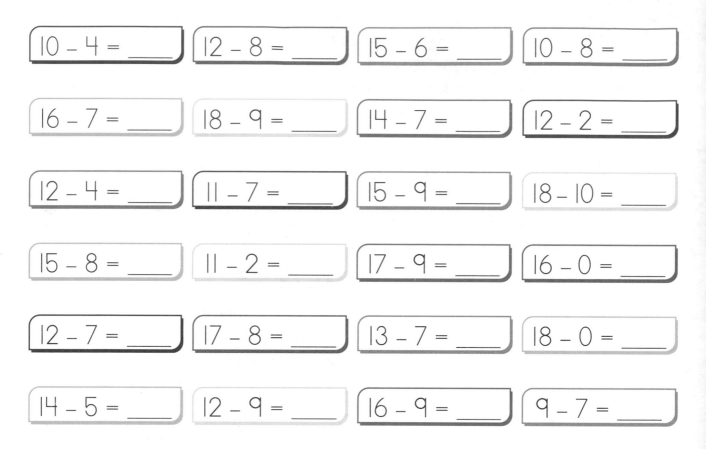

10 − 4 = _____　12 − 8 = _____　15 − 6 = _____　10 − 8 = _____

16 − 7 = _____　18 − 9 = _____　14 − 7 = _____　12 − 2 = _____

12 − 4 = _____　11 − 7 = _____　15 − 9 = _____　18 − 10 = _____

15 − 8 = _____　11 − 2 = _____　17 − 9 = _____　16 − 0 = _____

12 − 7 = _____　17 − 8 = _____　13 − 7 = _____　18 − 0 = _____

14 − 5 = _____　12 − 9 = _____　16 − 9 = _____　9 − 7 = _____

Subtraction

Word Problems

Read each subtraction word problem carefully and figure out the unknown number to solve the equation. Write that number on the line in each equation.

1. Avery has 10 students in her class. Some students went to the nurse. Now she has 3 students. How many children are not feeling well?

$$10 - \underline{\quad} = 3$$

2. Emily has 4 tomatoes. Lily has 8 tomatoes. How many fewer tomatoes does Emily have than Lily?

$$8 - 4 = \underline{\quad}$$

3. Connor has 9 tents. He has 3 brown tents and the rest are green. How many tents are green?

$$9 - 3 = \underline{\quad}$$

4. Trevor has some canoes for rent. He rents 2 out in the afternoon. Now he has 5 canoes. How many did he have in the morning?

$$\underline{\quad} - 2 = 5$$

Vertical Equations

Solve the subtraction equations. Write the differences below the equals lines.

$$12 - 2$$

$$12 - 3$$

$$10 - 1$$

$$11 - 4$$

$$12 - 5$$

$$10 - 2$$

$$9 - 4$$

$$12 - 7$$

$$8 - 5$$

$$11 - 1$$

$$10 - 8$$

$$7 - 6$$

$$12 - 4$$

$$9 - 3$$

$$8 - 4$$

$$4 - 0$$

$$12 - 6$$

$$5 - 2$$

$$9 - 8$$

$$6 - 4$$

$$12 - 8$$

$$5 - 4$$

Comparing Numbers

Comparing numbers means deciding how the numbers are different and categorizing them as more or less.

If a number is more, we say it is greater than the other number. If a number is less, we say it is less than the other number.

Look at the two numbers in each box below. Which number is the greater amount? Circle the greater amount.

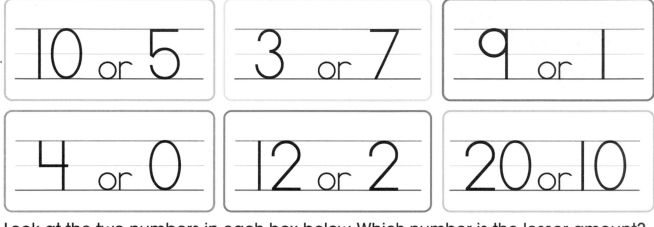

10 or 5   3 or 7   9 or 1

4 or 0   12 or 2   20 or 10

Look at the two numbers in each box below. Which number is the lesser amount? Circle the lesser amount.

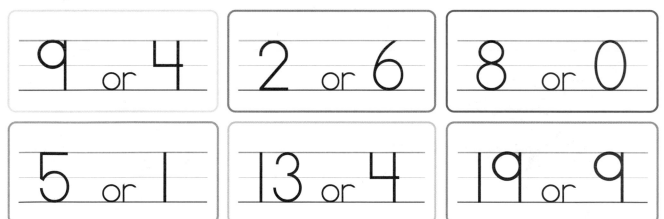

9 or 4   2 or 6   8 or 0

5 or 1   13 or 4   19 or 9

Comparing Numbers

The symbol for greater than is >.

The symbol for less than is <.

The symbol for equal to is =.

Equal to means the same amount as.

Sometimes using the greater than > and less than < symbols can be confusing! Try to remember that the open end of both symbols will face the greater amount.

Compare the amounts of objects in each row. Write the greater than > or less than < symbol in the circle based on the amount on the left side.

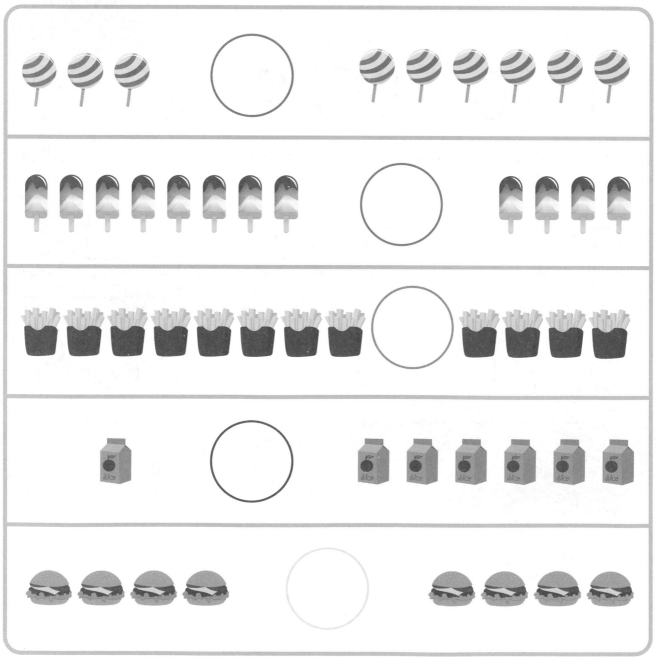

Equal Shares

Equal shares are parts of a whole. Equal shares must have the same size parts.
Example:

equal   not equal

Color the shapes below that have equal shares.

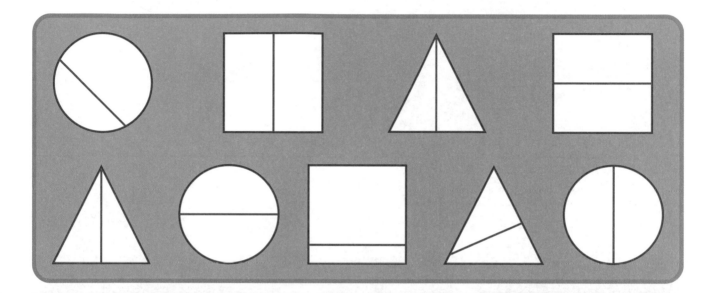

2 equal shares means dividing a whole into two equal parts.
Each part is 1 out of 2 parts of the whole.

Color the shapes below:
1 out of 2 parts - red
1 out of 2 parts - yellow

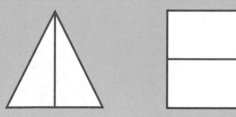 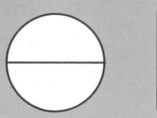

One Fourth

One fourth or $\frac{1}{4}$ means cutting a whole **into** four equal parts.
Each part is $\frac{1}{4}$ of the whole.

Color the shapes below:

1 out of 4 parts - red

1 out of 4 parts - yellow

1 out of 4 parts - blue

1 out of 4 parts - purple

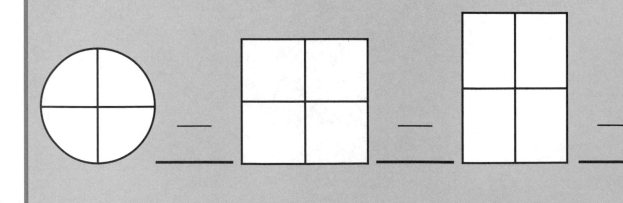

Place Value

Tens and Ones

Numbers with 2 digits have tens and ones.

The place of each digit tells which one it is.

Example: 15 = 1 ten and 5 ones.

The picture of ten blocks represent 1 bundle of ten.

The picture of five blocks represent 5 individual ones.

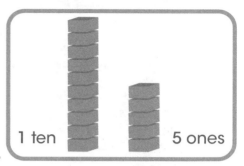

1 ten   5 ones

Look at the illustrations below and write how many tens and how many ones are in each group. Then, use those numbers to write the totals in the boxes.

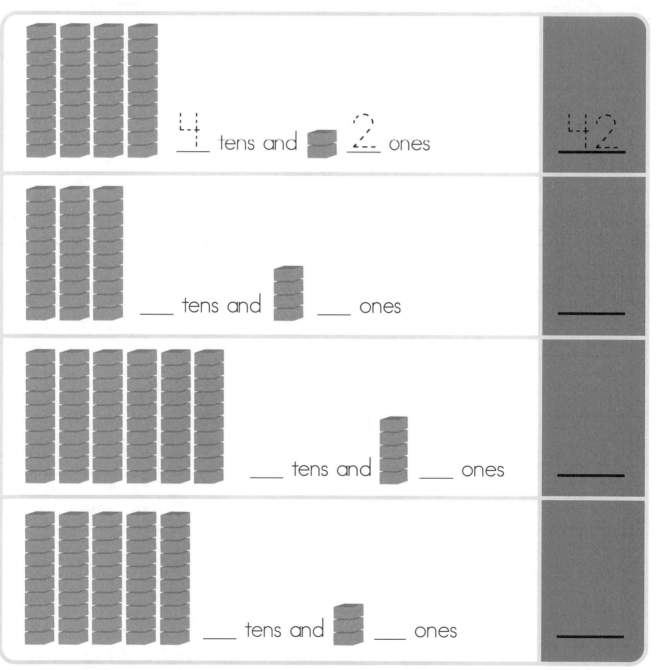

__4__ tens and __2__ ones   42

___ tens and ___ ones   ___

___ tens and ___ ones   ___

___ tens and ___ ones   ___

Place Value

Tens and Ones

Draw a line from each number to the matching tens and ones.

23	3 tens and 7 ones
37	2 tens and 3 ones
42	6 tens and 6 ones
63	4 tens and 2 ones
66	6 tens and 3 ones
76	9 tens and 1 one
91	7 tens and 6 ones
14	2 tens and 2 ones
22	1 ten and 4 ones
17	1 ten and 7 ones

Place Value

Tens and Ones

Write how many tens and ones are in each number on the lines below.

21 = ___ tens and ___ one

54 = ___ tens and ___ ones

15 = ___ ten and ___ ones

73 = ___ tens and ___ ones

24 = ___ tens and ___ ones

52 = ___ tens and ___ ones

42 = ___ tens and ___ ones

19 = ___ ten and ___ ones

81 = ___ tens and ___ one

11 = ___ ten and ___ one

66 = ___ tens and ___ ones

34 = ___ tens and ___ ones

53 = ___ tens and ___ ones

Length

We can measure the length of something in two ways.

We can use a nonstandard form of measurement, such as a paper clip or a stacking cube, or we can use a standard form of measurement, such as a ruler, which measures in inches.

Measure the items below with a nonstandard form of measurement and write the lengths on the lines below.

2 cubes

3

6

Measure the items below with a standard form of measurement and write the lengths on the lines below.

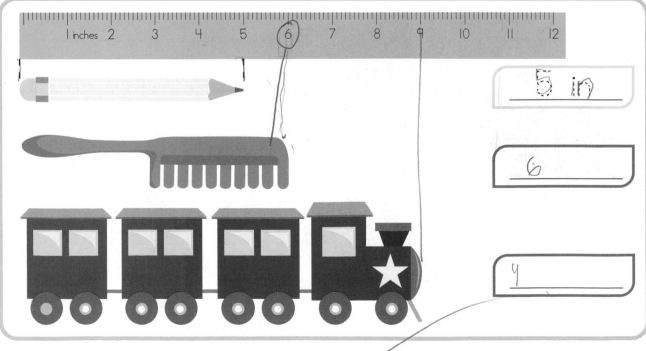

5 in

6

4

42

Longer and Shorter

Circle the objects that are longer. Cross out the objects that are shorter.

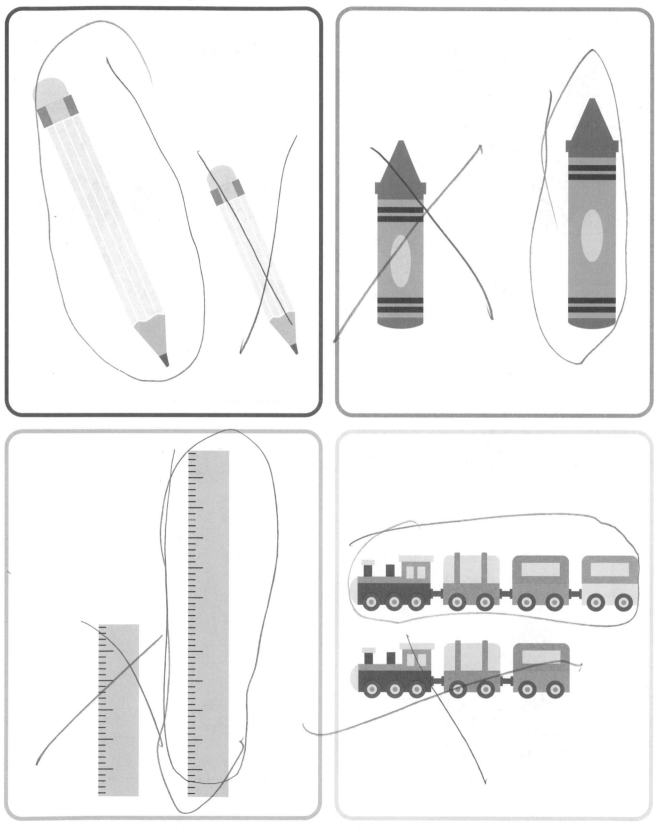

Measurement

Bigger and Smaller

Circle the objects that are bigger. Cross out the objects that are smaller.

Measurement

Heavier and Lighter

Circle the objects that are heavier. Cross out the objects that are lighter.

Comparing Sizes

Compare the pictures below.

Circle the taller.

Circle the smaller.

Circle the heavier.

Circle the bigger.

Circle the shorter.

Circle the longer.

Measurement

Capacity

Circle the objects below that hold more.

Cross out the objects that hold less.

  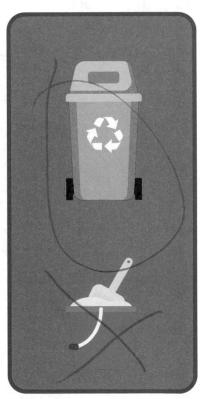

Clocks and Telling Time

Clocks can look different.

This is an analog clock.

It has a long hand and a short hand.

It has the numbers 1-12 on its face.

The long hand points to the minute and the short hand points to the hour. This clock says 5 o'clock.

45 minutes after the hour (quarter to)

30 minutes after the hour (half past)

This is a digital clock.

The first number shows the hour, and the second two numbers tell how many minutes after the hour it is. This clock says 3 o'clock.

3:00

hour   minutes

Write the digital time under each analog clock.

7:00   11:00   2:06

8:00   4:00   12:00

Time to the Hour

Write the digital time under each analog clock.

3

10

9

7

6

5

What time is it? Draw two hands on each clock to match the digital time.

2:00

12:00

4:00

5:00

8:00

7:00

Time to the Half Hour

Write the digital time under each analog clock.

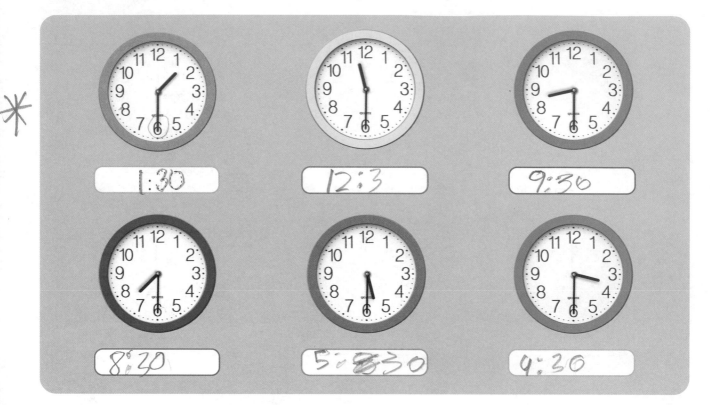

1:30   12:3   9:30

8:30   5:830   4:30

What time is it? Draw two hands on each analog clock to match the digital time.

2:30   4:30   6:30

8:00   10:00   12:30

Time

Time to the Hour and Half Hour

Draw a line to match the digital time to the analog clock.

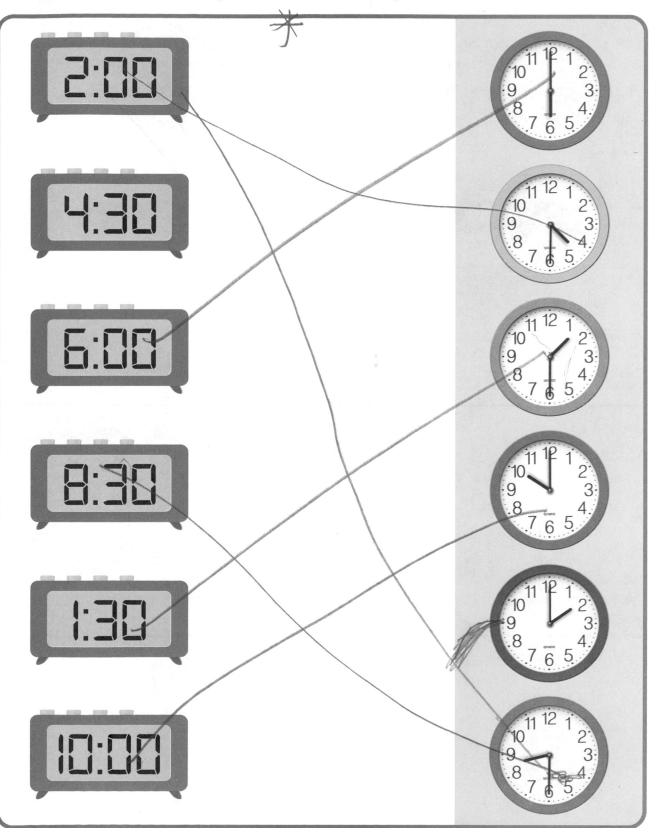

Calendars

There are 12 months in a year. April, June, September, and November all have 30 days. The other months have 31 days, except February. It is the shortest month with just 28 days.

Look at the calendar below. The days of the week are at the top of the month. The number of days in a month are called the dates. Fill in the missing dates in July.

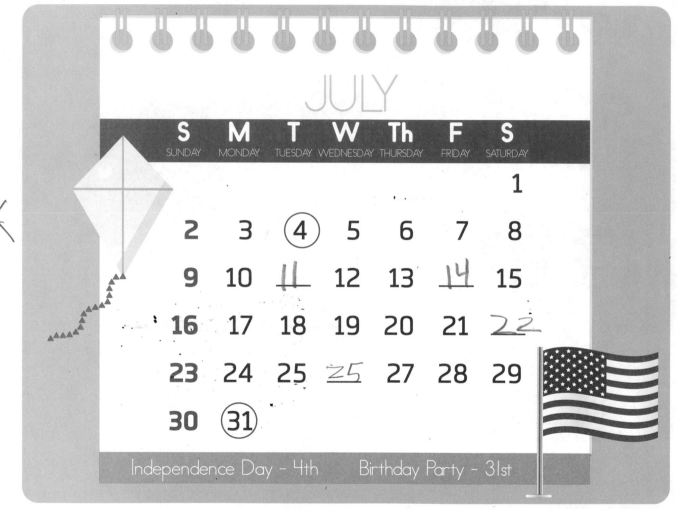

JULY

S SUNDAY	M MONDAY	T TUESDAY	W WEDNESDAY	Th THURSDAY	F FRIDAY	S SATURDAY
						1
2	3	(4)	5	6	7	8
9	10	11	12	13	14	15
16	17	18	19	20	21	22
23	24	25	25	27	28	29
30	(31)					

Independence Day - 4th   Birthday Party - 31st

Look at the calendar and answer the questions. Write your answers on the lines below.

Which month does this calendar show? _____

How many Fridays are in the month? _____

How many Saturdays are in the month? _____

How many days are in this month? _____

What is the date of the birthday party? _____

Geometry

3-Dimensional Shapes

3-D shapes are solid, not flat.
A sphere is like a bouncy ball.
A cube is like dice you roll.
A prism is like a tall building.
A cylinder is like a can of soda.
A cone is like a party hat.
3-D shapes are here and there.
3-D shapes are everywhere!

Color the 3-D shapes using the key below.

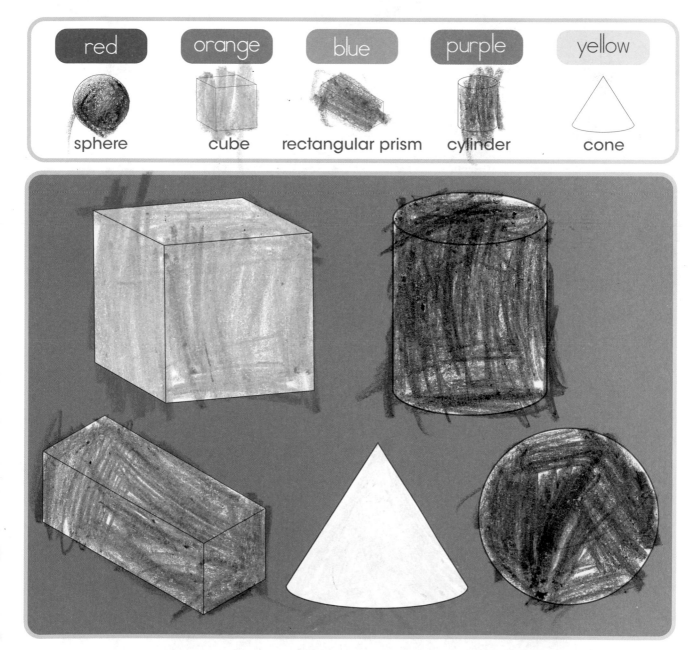

red	orange	blue	purple	yellow
sphere	cube	rectangular prism	cylinder	cone

Geometry

2-Dimensional and 3-Dimensional Shapes

Circle the 2-dimensional shapes with a red crayon.

Circle the 3-dimensional shapes with a blue crayon.

Making a Tally Mark Table

Tally marks can be used to show how many of each item there are.

Example: |||| = 4 and ʜʜ = 5 and ʜʜ | = 6

Count the fruit and fill in the graph using tally marks.

Fruit Market

Type of Fruit	Tally Marks	Number
Apple 5	ʜʜ	5
Orange 4		
Banana 6		
Watermelon 3		

Use the table to answer the questions below.

Which fruit has the least tally marks? _____

Which fruit has the most tally marks? _____

How many fruits are there in all? _____

Creating a Bar Graph

Each tally mark represents one insect.

Color in the number of units needed to match the tally marks for each insect on the bar graph.

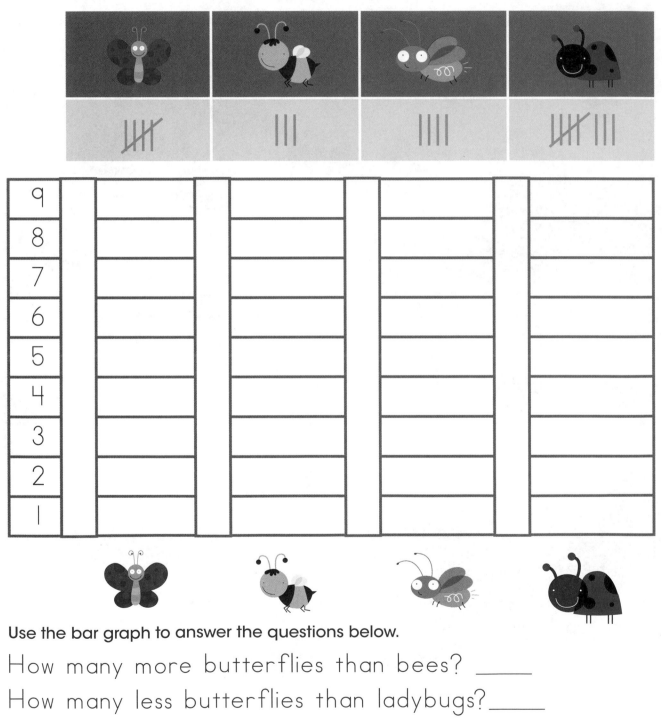

Summer Insects

Use the bar graph to answer the questions below.

How many more butterflies than bees? _____

How many less butterflies than ladybugs?_____

How many bees and fireflies are there all together?_____

56

Creating a Bar Graph

Each student in this first grade class picked their favorite treats. Complete the bar graph by coloring the correct number of boxes for each treat.

Our Favorite Treats

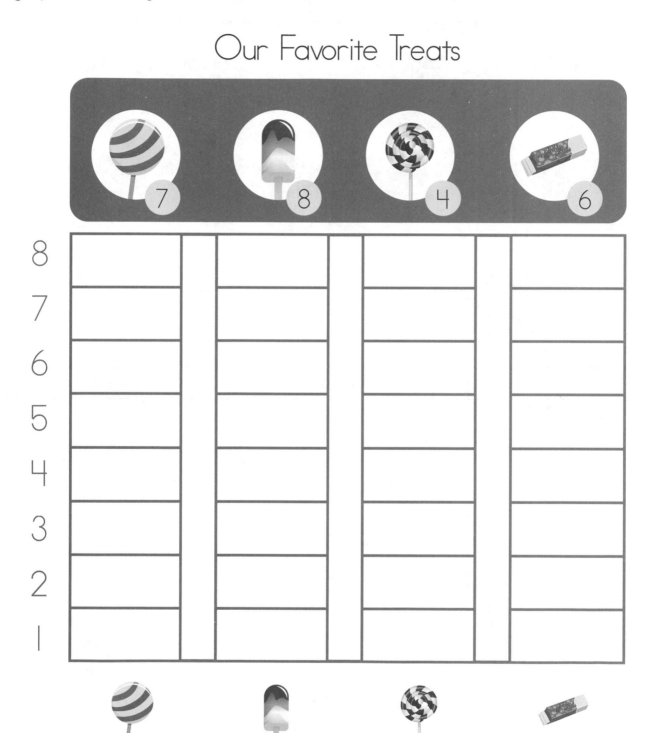

Which treat is the class favorite? _____

Graphing Shapes

Color in the graph to show how many of each shape is in the picture below.

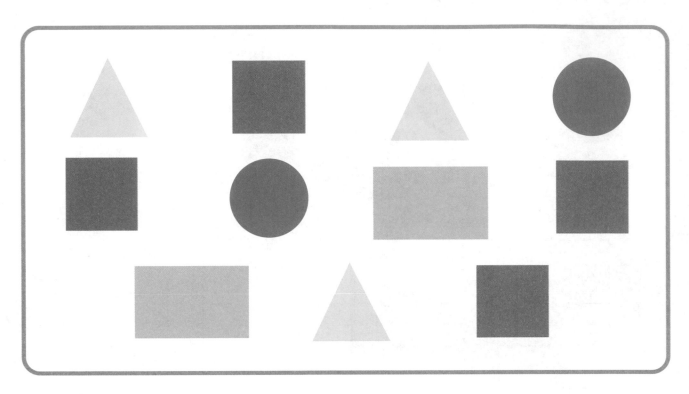

Shapes

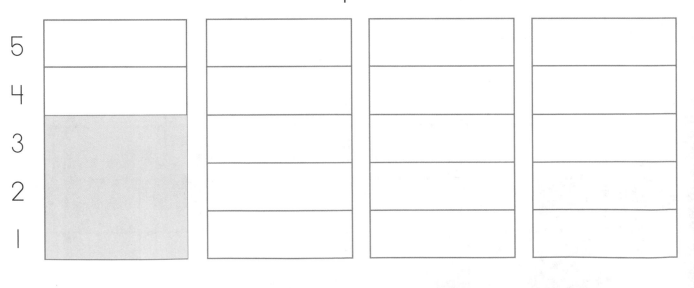

Sorting and Categorizing

Reading a Bar Graph

Each colored section represents one person who likes that sport. Count how many votes each sport received and answer the questions below.

How many people like football?_____

How many people like soccer?_____

How many people like basketball?_____

How many people like baseball?_____

Our Favorite Sports

ANSWER KEY

Page 4

Number Sense

Counting 1-10
Count the pictures in each box and write the total number on the lines below.

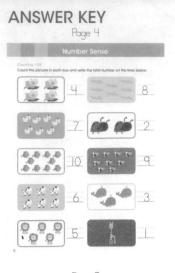

4 — 8
7 — 2
10 — 9
6 — 3
5 — 1

Page 6

Number Sense

Counting 11-20
Count the pictures in each box and write the total number on the lines below.

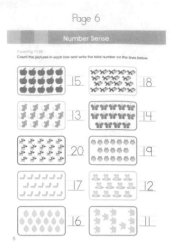

15 — 18
13 — 14
20 — 19
17 — 12
16 — 11

Page 7

Number Sense

Number Words
Draw a line from the number word to the matching number.

one — 3
two — 4
three — 1
four — 2
five — 7
six — 5
seven — 8
eight — 6
nine — 10
ten — 9

Page 9

Number Sense

Counting 51-100
Connect the dots from 51 to 100.
Color your new friend when you're finished.

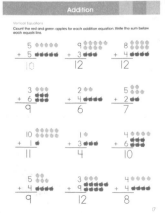

Page 11

Number Sense

Count by Twos
Skip counting can make counting faster! Skip counting means skipping numbers as you count.

Circle groups of 2 objects while you skip count the pictures in each row. Write the number on the lines for how many you counted in each row.

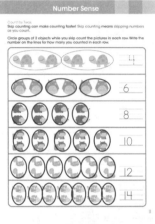

4
6
8
10
12
14

Page 13

Number Sense

Count by Tens
Count 10 objects at a time. Circle sets of 10 objects while you skip count the objects in each row. Write the number on the lines for how many you counted in each row.

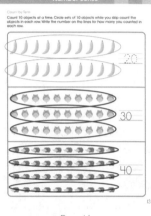

20
30
40

Page 14

Number Sense

Count by Tens
Count 10 objects at a time. Circle sets of 10 objects while you skip count the pictures in each row. Write the number on the lines for how many you counted in each row.

60
70
80
90

Page 15

Addition

Practice Addition
Count the objects in each box and write the numbers in the equations. Write the sum after the equals sign.

$2 + 3 = 5$
$4 + 2 = 6$
$3 + 5 = 8$
$6 + 1 = 7$
$7 + 2 = 9$
$3 + 3 = 6$
$4 + 5 = 9$
$1 + 8 = 9$

Page 16

Addition

Let's Play Dominoes!
Count the dots in each side of the domino and write the numbers in the equations. Write the sum after the equals sign.

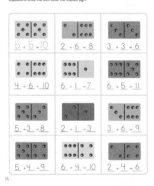

$5 + 5 = 10$ $2 + 6 = 8$ $3 + 3 = 6$
$4 + 6 = 10$ $6 + 1 = 7$ $6 + 5 = 11$
$5 + 3 = 8$ $2 + 1 = 3$ $3 + 6 = 9$
$5 + 4 = 9$ $6 + 4 = 10$ $2 + 4 = 6$

Page 17

Addition

Vertical Equations
Count the red and green apples for each addition equation. Write the sum below each equals line.

$5 + 5 = 10$ $9 + 3 = 12$ $8 + 4 = 12$

$3 + 6 = 9$ $2 + 4 = 6$ $5 + 2 = 7$

$10 + 1 = 11$ $1 + 3 = 4$ $4 + 6 = 10$

$5 + 4 = 9$ $3 + 9 = 12$ $4 + 4 = 8$

Page 18

Addition

Using a Number Line
You can use a number line to help you count when adding.

Start on the number line at the first number in the equation. Then jump forward the number of spaces for the amount being added to the first number. Circle the number on this number line where the jump line ends. This is the sum. Write the sum after the equals sign.

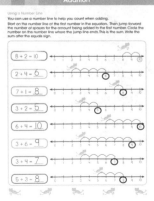

$8 + 2 = 10$
$2 + 4 = 6$
$7 + 1 = 8$
$3 + 2 = 5$
$6 + 4 = 10$
$3 + 6 = 9$
$3 + 4 = 7$
$5 + 3 = 8$

Page 19

Addition

Using a Number Line
Start on the first number in the equation. Then jump forward on the line the same number of spaces as the second number. Draw a line from the first number to the second number and circle the correct answer. Then write the answers to the equations on the lines below.

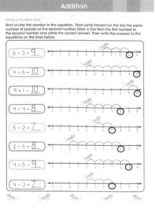

$6 + 3 = 9$
$4 + 6 = 10$
$9 + 1 = 10$
$4 + 4 = 8$
$5 + 2 = 7$
$2 + 6 = 8$
$4 + 5 = 9$
$4 + 3 = 7$

Page 20

Addition

Sunny Summer Math

Solve the addition equations and write the sums on the lines below. Then color the pictures.

$4 + 8 = 12$	$4 + 6 = 10$	$5 + 6 = 11$
$9 + 3 = 12$	$6 + 6 = 12$	$5 + 7 = 12$
$9 + 1 = 10$	$5 + 1 = 6$	$8 + 3 = 11$
$7 + 5 = 12$	$9 + 2 = 11$	$7 + 4 = 11$
$6 + 2 = 8$	$1 + 6 = 7$	$6 + 3 = 9$	$10 + 2 = 12$
$11 + 1 = 12$	$4 + 4 = 8$	$8 + 5 = 13$	$3 + 8 = 11$

Page 21

Addition

Word Problems

Sometimes math equations are hidden in word problems. Read each addition word problem carefully and figure out the unknown number to solve the equation. Write that number on the line in each equation.

Example: Maddy has ②red beads. She gets ③more beads from a friend. How many beads does Maddy have now?

$2 + 3 = 5$ ●● + ●●●

Circle the clues and solve the word problems. Write your answers on the lines below.

1. Lucy has a seashell collection. She was given ③ more seashells. Now she has ⑩ seashells. How many seashells did she have before she got some more?

$7 + 3 = 10$

2. Emma invited ⑩ children to her party. Some girls and boys came. How many girls were invited?

$5 + 5 = 10$

3. Sophia likes to run. She ran ④ miles on Monday and ⑥ miles on Tuesday. How far did she run in two days?

$4 + 6 = 10$

4. Noah has ② toy trucks. Luke has ⑦ toy trucks. How many more toy trucks does Luke have than Noah?

$2 + 5 = 7$

Page 22

Addition

Add to the Fun

Solve the addition problems. Write the answers below.

$\begin{array}{r}2\\+0\\\hline2\end{array}$	$\begin{array}{r}3\\+1\\\hline4\end{array}$	$\begin{array}{r}6\\+2\\\hline8\end{array}$	$\begin{array}{r}3\\+2\\\hline5\end{array}$	$\begin{array}{r}5\\+2\\\hline7\end{array}$
$\begin{array}{r}7\\+1\\\hline8\end{array}$	$\begin{array}{r}6\\+3\\\hline9\end{array}$	$\begin{array}{r}9\\+1\\\hline10\end{array}$	$\begin{array}{r}6\\+5\\\hline11\end{array}$	$\begin{array}{r}10\\+2\\\hline12\end{array}$
$\begin{array}{r}5\\+7\\\hline12\end{array}$	$\begin{array}{r}8\\+3\\\hline11\end{array}$	$\begin{array}{r}4\\+5\\\hline9\end{array}$	$\begin{array}{r}0\\+7\\\hline7\end{array}$	$\begin{array}{r}5\\+4\\\hline9\end{array}$
$\begin{array}{r}8\\+4\\\hline12\end{array}$	$\begin{array}{r}3\\+7\\\hline10\end{array}$			
$\begin{array}{r}7\\+5\\\hline12\end{array}$	$\begin{array}{r}5\\+5\\\hline10\end{array}$			
$\begin{array}{r}8\\+1\\\hline9\end{array}$	$\begin{array}{r}4\\+1\\\hline5\end{array}$			

Page 23

Addition

Word Problems

Read each addition word problem carefully and figure out the unknown number to solve the equation. Write that number on the line in each equation.

1. Sarah has 5 test tubes. She has 3 red and the rest are red. How many test tubes are red?

$3 + 2 = 5$

2. Lauren has 4 T-shirts with a red heart on them. She has 5 T-shirts with a dog on them. How many T-shirts does she own?

$4 + 5 = 9$

3. Ashley has 8 shoes. She has 6 shoes with laces and the rest have buttons. How many shoes have buttons?

$6 + 2 = 8$

4. Kim painted all 10 of her nails. She painted 3 pink and the rest she painted blue. How many nails did she paint blue?

$7 + 3 = 10$

Page 25

Subtraction

Practice Subtraction

Subtracting is taking away part of a whole number.
When we use pictures to subtract, we start with the whole number and then cross out the number of objects we are subtracting.

Example: $6 - 2 = 4$

Count the total number of objects in each row. Count backward for the amount of the second number in the equation, starting from the right. (this will be the X objects). The number of objects left is the difference. Write the difference under the equals line.

$\begin{array}{r}8\\-4\\\hline4\end{array}$

$\begin{array}{r}9\\-6\\\hline3\end{array}$

$\begin{array}{r}10\\-6\\\hline4\end{array}$

$\begin{array}{r}7\\-4\\\hline4\end{array}$

$\begin{array}{r}5\\-1\\\hline4\end{array}$

$\begin{array}{r}8\\-2\\\hline6\end{array}$

Page 26

Subtraction

Practice Subtraction

Cross out the number of objects you are subtracting from the total. Count the objects left and write the difference after the equals sign.

$9 - 3 = 6$	$10 - 4 = 6$
$7 - 6 = 1$	$12 - 7 = 5$
$9 - 7 = 2$	$14 - 10 = 4$
$6 - 3 = 3$	$11 - 8 = 3$

Page 27

Subtraction

Practice Subtraction

Cross out the number of objects you are subtracting from the total. Count the objects left and write the difference after the equals sign.

$8 - 3 = 5$	$5 - 4 = 1$
$7 - 5 = 2$	$9 - 2 = 7$
$6 - 3 = 3$	$8 - 5 = 3$
$7 - 2 = 5$	$6 - 2 = 4$

Page 28

Subtraction

Let's Play Dominoes!

Use the dots on the dominoes to help you subtract. Write the difference for each equation after the equals sign.

$12 - 6 = 6$	$9 - 4 = 5$	$10 - 6 = 4$
$11 - 6 = 5$	$8 - 2 = 6$	$6 - 3 = 3$
$7 - 1 = 6$	$10 - 5 = 5$	$8 - 5 = 3$
$7 - 3 = 4$	$8 - 4 = 4$	$6 - 2 = 4$

Page 29

Subtraction

Word Problems

Sometimes math equations are hidden in word problems. Read each subtraction word problem carefully and figure out the unknown number to solve the equation. Write that number on the line in each equation.

Example: Maddy said there were ⑤ apples on the table. She ate some. Now there are ② apples. How many did Maddy eat?

$5 - 3 = 2$

Circle the clues and solve the word problems. Write your answers on the lines below.

1. Juan has ⑤ trading cards. He gave ② away as gifts. How many does he still have?

$5 - 2 = 3$

2. Oliver popped ④ balloons at the party. Mason popped ⑧ balloons. How many fewer balloons did Oliver pop than Mason?

$8 - 4 = 4$

3. Logan has some drums on Monday. He gave ⑤ drums away on Tuesday. Now he has ④ drums. How many drums did he have on Monday?

$9 - 5 = 4$

4. Hannah has ④ fewer sheep than Riley. Riley has ⑦ sheep. How many sheep does Hannah have?

$7 - 4 = 3$

Page 30

Subtraction

Using a Number Line

You can use a number line to help you count when subtracting.
Start on the number line at the first number in the equation. Then, jump backward the number of spaces for the amount being taken away from the first number. Circle the number on the number line where the jump line ends. This is the difference. Write the difference after the equals sign.

Example

$9 - 6 = 3$

$6 - 2 = 4$

$5 - 4 = 1$

$4 - 1 = 3$

$3 - 3 = 0$

$6 - 5 = 1$

$4 - 4 = 0$

$7 - 5 = 2$

$9 - 2 = 7$

Page 31

Subtraction

Using a Number Line

Start on the number line at the first number in the equation. Then, jump backward the number of spaces for the amount being taken away from the first number. Circle the number on the number line where the jump line ends. This is the difference. Write the difference after the equals sign.

$7 - 6 = 1$

$8 - 6 = 2$

$8 - 7 = 1$

$9 - 7 = 2$

$7 - 2 = 5$

$9 - 5 = 4$

$5 - 2 = 3$

$6 - 2 = 4$

$8 - 1 = 7$

Page 32

Subtraction

Math Can Be a Picnic!

Solve the subtraction equations and write the differences after the equals signs.

$10 - 4 = 6$	$12 - 8 = 4$	$15 - 6 = 9$	$10 - 8 = 2$
$16 - 7 = 9$	$18 - 9 = 9$	$14 - 7 = 7$	$12 - 2 = 10$
$12 - 4 = 8$	$11 - 7 = 4$	$15 - 9 = 6$	$18 - 10 = 8$
$15 - 8 = 7$	$11 - 2 = 9$	$17 - 9 = 8$	$16 - 0 = 16$
$12 - 7 = 5$	$17 - 8 = 9$	$13 - 7 = 6$	$18 - 0 = 18$
$14 - 5 = 9$	$12 - 9 = 3$	$16 - 9 = 7$	$9 - 7 = 2$

Page 33

Subtraction

Word Problems
Read each subtraction word problem carefully and figure out the unknown number to solve the equation. Write that number on the line in each equation.

1. Avery has 10 students in her class. Some students went to the nurse. Now she has 3 students. How many children are not feeling well?

10 - _7_ = 3

2. Emily has 4 tomatoes. Lily has 8 tomatoes. How many fewer tomatoes does Emily have than Lily?

8 - 4 = _4_

3. Connor has 9 tents. He has 3 brown tents and the rest are green. How many tents are green?

9 - 3 = _6_

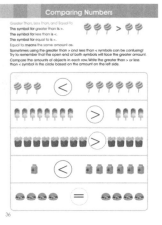

4. Trevor has some canoes for rent. He rents 2 out in the afternoon. Now he has 5 canoes. How many did he have in the morning?

_7_ - 2 = 5

Page 34

Subtraction

Vertical Equations
Solve the subtraction equations. Write the differences below the equals lines.

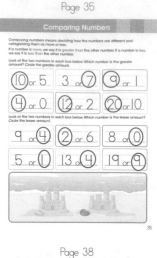

12	12	10	11	12
− 2	− 3	− 1	− 4	− 5
10	9	9	7	7

10	9	8	11	12
− 2	− 1	− 3	− 1	− 2
8	8	5	10	10

10	7	12		8
− 8	− 1	− 4		− 4
2	6	8		4

4	8	5	6
− 0	− 6	− 2	− 4
4	2	3	2

12	5
− 8	− 4
4	1

Page 35

Comparing Numbers

Comparing numbers means deciding how the numbers are different and categorizing them as more or less.
If a number is more, we say it is greater than the other number. If a number is less, we say it is less than the other number.

Look at the two numbers in each box below. Which number is the greater amount? Circle the greater amount.

(10) or 5   3 or (7)   (9) or 1
(4) or 0   (12) or 2   (20) or 10

Look at the two numbers in each box below. Which number is the lesser amount? Circle the lesser amount.

9 or (4)   (2) or 6   8 or (0)
5 or (0)   13 or (4)   19 or (9)

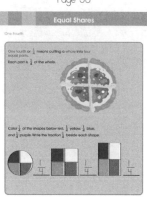

Page 36

Comparing Numbers

Greater Than, Less Than, and Equal to
The symbol for greater than is >.
The symbol for less than is <.
The symbol for equal to is =.
Equal to means the same amount as.
Sometimes using the greater than > and less than < symbols can be confusing! Try to remember that the open end of both symbols will face the greater amount.
Compare the amounts of objects in each row. Write the greater than > or less than < symbol in the circle based on the amount on the left side.

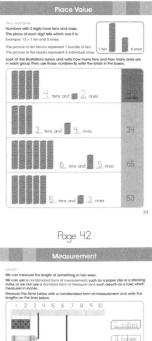

(<)
(>)
(>)
(<)
(=)

Page 37

Equal Shares

Equal Shares
Equal shares are parts of a whole. Equal shares must be the same size.
Example:

equal   not equal

Color the shapes below that have equal shares.

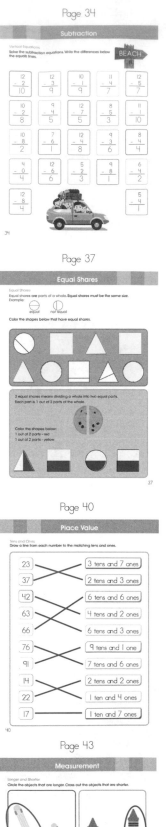

2 equal shares means dividing a whole into two equal parts. Each part is 1 out of 2 parts of the whole.

Color the shapes below:
1 out of 2 parts - red
1 out of 2 parts - yellow

Page 38

Equal Shares

One Fourth

One fourth or $\frac{1}{4}$ means cutting a whole into four equal parts.
Each part is $\frac{1}{4}$ of the whole.

Color $\frac{1}{4}$ of the shapes below red, $\frac{1}{4}$ yellow, $\frac{1}{4}$ blue, and $\frac{1}{4}$ purple. Write the fraction $\frac{1}{4}$ beside each shape.

$\frac{1}{4}$ $\frac{1}{4}$ $\frac{1}{4}$

Page 39

Place Value

Tens and Ones
Numbers with 2 digits have tens and ones.
The place of each digit tells which one it is.
Example: 15 > 1 ten and 5 ones.
The picture of ten blocks represent 1 bundle of ten.
The picture of five blocks represent 5 individual ones.
Look at the illustrations below and write how many tens and how many ones are in each group. Then, use those numbers to write the totals in the boxes.

_4_ tens and _2_ ones   42
_3_ tens and _4_ ones   34
_6_ tens and _5_ ones   65
_5_ tens and _3_ ones   53

Page 40

Place Value

Tens and Ones
Draw a line from each number to the matching tens and ones.

23		3 tens and 7 ones
37		2 tens and 3 ones
42		6 tens and 6 ones
63		4 tens and 2 ones
66		6 tens and 3 ones
76		9 tens and 1 one
91		7 tens and 6 ones
14		2 tens and 2 ones
22		1 ten and 4 ones
17		1 ten and 7 ones

Page 41

Place Value

Tens and Ones
Write how many tens and ones are in each number on the lines below.

21 = _2_ tens and _1_ one   54 = _5_ tens and _4_ ones
15 = _1_ ten and _5_ ones   73 = _7_ tens and _3_ ones
24 = _2_ tens and _4_ ones   52 = _5_ tens and _2_ ones
42 = _4_ tens and _2_ ones   19 = _1_ ten and _9_ ones
81 = _8_ tens and _1_ one   11 = _1_ ten and _1_ one
66 = _6_ tens and _6_ ones   34 = _3_ tens and _4_ ones
53 = _5_ tens and _3_ ones

Page 42

Measurement

Length
We can measure the length of something in two ways.
We can use a nonstandard form of measurement, such as a paper clip or a stacking cube, or we can use a standard form of measurement, such as such as a ruler, which measures in inches.
Measure the items below with a nonstandard form of measurement and write the lengths on the lines below.

2 cubes
3 cubes
6 cubes

Measure the items below with a standard form of measurement and write the lengths on the lines below.

5 in
6 in
9 in

Page 43

Measurement

Longer and Shorter
Circle the objects that are longer. Cross out the objects that are shorter.

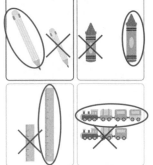

Page 44

Measurement

Bigger and Smaller
Circle the objects that are bigger. Cross out the objects that are smaller.

Page 45
Measurement
Heavier and Lighter
Circle the objects that are heavier. Cross out the objects that are lighter.

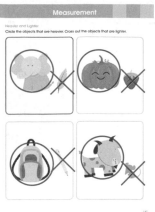

Page 46
Measurement
Comparing Sizes
Compare the pictures below.

Circle the taller. / Circle the smaller.
Circle the heavier. / Circle the bigger.
Circle the shorter. / Circle the longer.

Page 47
Measurement
Capacity
Circle the objects below that hold more.

Cross out the objects that hold less.

Page 48
Time
Clocks and Telling Time
Clocks can look different.
This is an analog clock.
It has a long hand and a short hand.
It has the numbers 1-12 on its face.
The long hand points to the minute and the short hand points to the hour. This clock says 5 o'clock.

This is a digital clock.
The first number shows the hour, and the second two numbers tell how many minutes after the hour it is.
This clock says 3 o'clock.

3:00

Write the digital time under each analog clock.

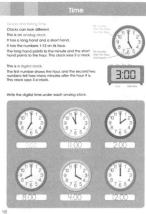

Page 49
Time
Time to the Hour
Write the digital time under each analog clock.

3:00 / 10:00 / 9:00
1:00 / 6:00 / 5:00

What time is it? Draw two hands on each clock to match the digital time.

2:00 / 12:00 / 4:00
5:00 / 8:00 / 7:00

Page 50
Time
Time to the Half Hour
Write the digital time under each analog clock.

1:30 / 11:30 / 8:30
7:30 / 5:30 / 3:30

What time is it? Draw two hands on each analog clock to match the digital time.

Page 51
Time
Time to the Hour and Half Hour
Draw a line to match the digital time to the analog clock.

2:00
4:30
6:00
8:30
1:30
10:00

Page 52
Time
Calendar
There are 12 months in a year. April, June, September, and November all have 30 days. The other months have 31 days, except February. It is the shortest month with just 28 days.

Look at the calendar below. The days of the week are at the top of the month. The number of days in a month are called the dates. Fill in the missing dates in July.

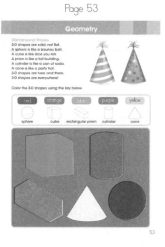

JULY

S	M	T	W	Th	F	S
						1
2	3	4	5	6	7	8
9	10	11	12	13	14	15
16	17	18	19	20	21	22
23	24	25	26	27	28	29
30	31					

Look at the calendar and answer the questions. Write your answers on the lines below.

Which month does the calendar show?	July
How many Fridays are in the month?	4
How many Saturdays are in the month?	5
How many days are in the month?	31
What is the date of the birthday party?	31st

Page 53
Geometry
3-Dimensional Shapes
3-D shapes are solid, not flat.
A sphere is like a bouncy ball.
A cube is like dice you roll.
A prism is like a tall building.
A cylinder is like a can of soda.
A cone is like a party hat.
3-D shapes are here and there.
3-D shapes are everywhere!

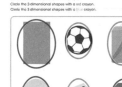

Color the 3-D shapes using the key below.

| red | orange | blue | purple | yellow |
| sphere | cube | rectangular prism | cylinder | cone |

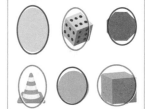

Page 54
Geometry
2-Dimensional and 3-Dimensional Shapes
Circle the 2-dimensional shapes with a red crayon.
Circle the 3-dimensional shapes with a blue crayon.

Page 55
Data Graphing and Analysis
Making a Tally Mark Table
Tally marks can be used to show how many of each item there are.
Count the fruit and fill in the graph using tally marks.

Fruit Market

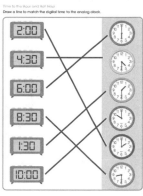

Type of Fruit	Tally Marks	Number
Apple	||||	5
Orange	||||	4
Banana	||||		6
Watermelon	|||	3

Use the table to answer the questions below.
Which fruit has the least tally marks? Watermelon
Which fruit has the most tally marks? Banana
How many fruits are there in all? 18

Page 56
Data Graphing and Analysis
Creating a Bar Graph
Each tally mark represents one insect.
Color in the number of units needed to match the tally marks for each insect on the bar graph.

Summer Insects

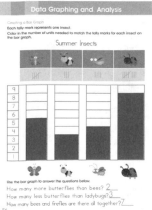

Use the bar graph to answer the questions below.
How many more butterflies than bees? 2
How many less butterflies than ladybugs? 3
How many bees and fireflies are there all together? 7

Page 57
Data Graphing and Analysis
Creating a Bar Graph
Each student in this first grade class picked their favorite treats. Complete the bar graph by coloring the correct number of boxes for each treat.

Our Favorite Treats

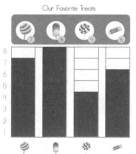

Which treat is the class favorite? Popsicle

Page 58
Sorting and Categorizing
Graphing Shapes
Color in the graph to show how many of each shape is in the picture below.

Shapes

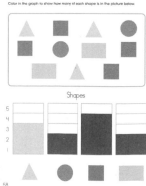

Page 59
Sorting and Categorizing
Reading a Bar Graph
Each colored section represents one person who likes that sport. Count how many votes each sport received and answer the questions below.

How many people like football? 6
How many people like soccer? 3
How many people like basketball? 5
How many people like baseball? 9

Our Favorite Sports

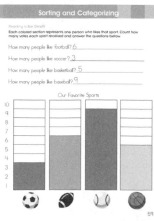

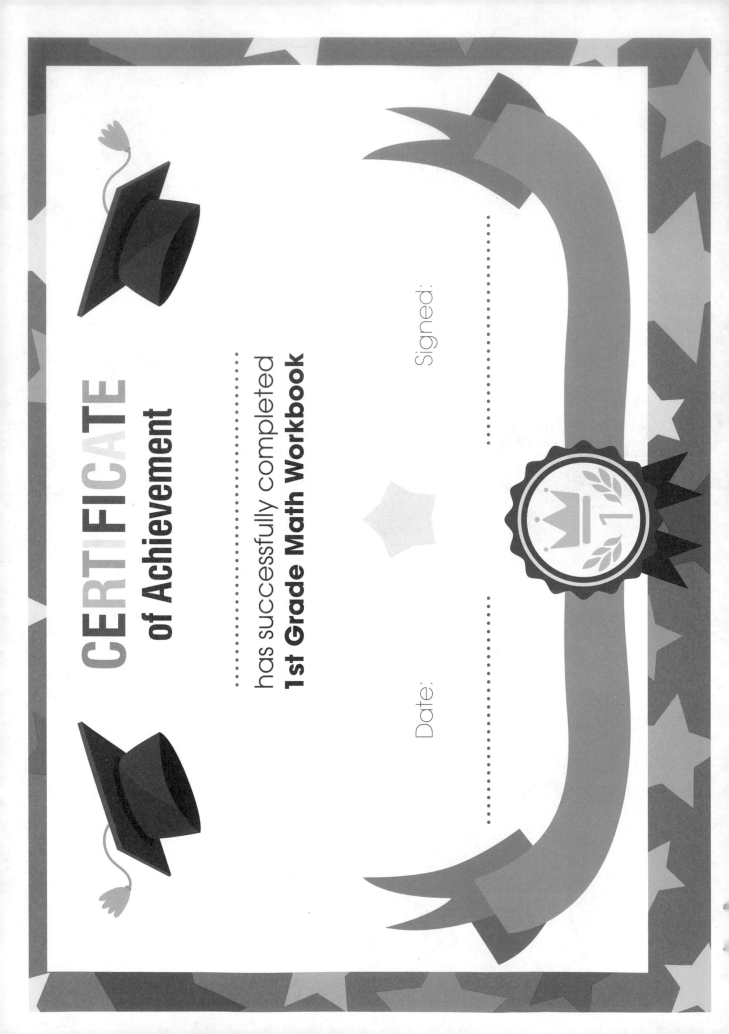

CERTIFICATE
of Achievement

has succesfully completed
1st Grade Math Workbook

Date:

Signed: